Contents

Lewis and Clark

In May 1804, a daring **expedition** set out from St Louis, USA. It was led by two men, Meriwether Lewis and William Clark. Their mission was to find a river route from St Louis, Missouri, across western USA to the Pacific Ocean. Large parts of this region had never been explored before.

Meriwether Lewis

Lewis was born on 18 August 1774 in the state of Virginia, USA. As a boy, he was fascinated by nature and liked being outdoors. In 1795, Lewis joined the army and rose to the rank of captain. Six years later, he became **private secretary** to the US president, Thomas Jefferson. It was Jefferson who chose Lewis to lead the expedition to the Pacific.

Lewis and Clark's journey

Map labels: Oregon County · Fort Clatsop · Claimed by U.S. and Great Britain · Indiana Territory · New Spain · St. Louis · United · Louisiana Purchase · Claimed by U.S. and Spain

Legend:
Outward journey
Homeward journey
- - Lewis
..... Clark

4

1 August 1770
Clark born

18 August 1774
Lewis born

1780
Clark joins the army

SURVIVAL!

Anita Ganeri

Published 2011
First published in hardback 2010 by
A&C Black Publishers Ltd.
36 Soho Square, London, W1D 3QY

www.acblack.com

ISBN 978-1-4081-2682-0

Series consultant: Gill Matthews

This book is produced using paper that is made from wood grown in managed, sustainable forests. It is natural, renewable and recyclable. The logging and manufacturing processes conform to the environmental regulations of the country of origin.

Produced for A&C Black by Calcium. www.calciumcreative.co.uk

Printed and bound in China by C&C Offset Printing Co.

All the internet addresses given in this book were correct at the time of going to press. The author and publishers regret any inconvenience caused if addresses have changed or sites have ceased to exist, but can accept no responsibility for any such changes.

Acknowledgements

The publishers would like to thank the following for their kind permission to reproduce their photographs:

Cover: Shutterstock except The Pepin Press/Agile Rabbit Editions, (br) Blue Lantern Studio/Corbis.
Pages: Corbis: Bettmann 8; Library of Congress: 6, 11, 12, 17, 18; Photolibrary: North Wind Picture Archives 28; Rex Features: c.JTavin/Everett 5r; Shutterstock: Wesley Aston 21, Flashon Studio 24, Tom Grundy 19, Hasanugurlu 7b, John Kropewnicki 26, Timothy Lee Lantgen 13, Stephen Mcsweeny 15, Pix2go 9, Denton Rumsey 23, B.G. Smith 14, Vladimir Wrangel 26b, Artem Zhushman 7t; U.S Army: Fort Clatsop National Memorial Collection 20; Wikimedia Commons: 22, George Catlin/Cliff1066 5l, Cliff1066 16, Library of Congress 10, 25, Charles Willson Peale 27; WPClipart 29.

William Clark
(1770–1838)
and Meriwether
Lewis (1774–1809)

WHAT THEY SAID:

William Clark

For his co-leader, Lewis chose his army friend, William Clark. Clark was born on 1 August 1770, also in Virginia. His family later settled in Kentucky where he learned outdoor survival skills from his older brothers. He followed in his brothers' footsteps and joined the army, where he met Lewis.

"Your mission is to explore the Missouri River [to] the waters of the Pacific Ocean [to find] the most direct and practicable water communication across this continent, for the purposes of commerce."

President Thomas Jefferson

1795
Lewis joins the army

1801
Lewis becomes private secretary to President Jefferson

Getting Ready

Lewis and Clark spent much of 1803 getting ready for their expedition. They studied useful subjects, such as **navigation**, medicine, and **biology**. They also looked at the maps and diaries of traders who had already travelled part of the way.

Corps of Discovery

Many people wanted to join the expedition. Lewis and Clark chose about 45 of them. There were soldiers, hunters, **blacksmiths**, carpenters, and an **interpreter** to help them speak with the **Native American** tribes they met. Lewis also took along his faithful Newfoundland dog, Seaman. They called the team the "Corps of Discovery".

Lewis and Clark met many Native Americans on their journey.

January 1803	Spring 1803	Spring 1803
Jefferson secretly plans the expedition	Jefferson chooses Lewis to lead the expedition	Lewis asks Clark to join the expedition

Winter camp

In Pittsburgh, Lewis supervized the building of the expedition's 18-metre (60 ft) long **keelboat**. Then Clark sailed the boat to Camp Dubois, at the meeting point of the Mississippi and Missouri Rivers. This was where the Corps spent the winter. The following spring, Lewis went ahead to St Louis to collect supplies. A few days later, Clark and the rest of the Corps set off down the river to join him.

Knives were useful expedition tools.

HIGHLIGHTS

Among the expedition's supplies were:
- camping equipment
- clothing
- medicines
- scientific instruments
- weapons

Gifts for the Native Americans:
- mirrors
- scissors
- ribbons
- tobacco
- knives

Setting Off

On 20 May 1804, the expedition finally left St Louis and followed the Missouri River westwards. Lewis and Clark's journey into the unknown had begun.

River transport

The Corps and all of their equipment were loaded into three boats – the keelboat and two canoes, one large and one small. Each boat had sails and oars. Clark spent most of his time in the keelboat, charting their course and making maps. Meanwhile, Lewis often went ashore to look at rocks, animals, and plants.

Lewis and Clark sailed along the Missouri River.

14 May 1804

The Corps leaves
Camp Dubois

20 May 1804

The Corps
leaves St Louis

Beavers were hunted for food and for their fur.

Summer journey

It was a long, hot summer and sailing upriver was hard work. Sometimes, their way was blocked by tree trunks and **sandbars**. The men caught **dysentery** and were also badly bitten by mosquitoes. Despite this, they hunted deer, beavers, birds, and fish for food, and made good progress. By the end of July, they had covered more than 1,000 kilometres (more than 600 miles).

WHAT THEY SAID:

"The party is much afflicted with boils and several have dysentery [from] the water. The country about this place is beautiful... and abounds in deer, **elk**, and bear. The ticks and mosquitoes are very troublesome."

Clark's diary, 17 July 1804

4 July 1804	21 July 1804	End July 1804
The Corps celebrates Independence Day	The Corps reaches the Platte River	The Corps have covered more than 1,000 km

Many Meetings

As Lewis and Clark travelled along the river, they met many tribes of Native Americans. These meetings were mostly friendly, but not always.

Council Bluff

In early August, the expedition reached the lands of the Oto and Missouri Indian tribes. These tribes lived by farming and hunting buffalo. At a place called Council Bluff, Lewis and Clark met the chiefs of the tribes and gave them gifts, including peace medals and face paints.

The Corps found Oto tribespeople to be friendly.

3 August 1804
The meeting at Council Bluff

20 August 1804
Captain Charles Floyd dies of natural causes

Quarrel with the Sioux

The Oto and Missouri were friendly but Lewis and Clark then entered Sioux territory. The Sioux did not want the gifts that Lewis and Clark offered. Instead, their chief demanded one of the expedition's boats as payment for letting them travel upriver. Both sides got ready to fight but, at the last moment, Chief Black Buffalo called his men off. Disaster was avoided, and the expedition went on its way quickly.

Sioux warriors on horseback were quite a menacing sight.

HIGHLIGHTS

Lewis and Clark discovered many new plants and animals that they had never seen before. These included squirrel-like **rodents**, called prairie dogs, which live in huge groups. A live prairie dog was caught and sent back to President Jefferson.

A Bitter Winter

After fleeing from their **skirmish** with the Sioux, Lewis and Clark carried on up the river. Winter was drawing in and the weather was beginning to get colder.

Fort Mandan

In October 1804, they stopped at a village belonging to the Mandan tribe where the chief gave them a warm welcome. They decided to spend the winter there, and ordered their men to build a small fort and log cabins nearby. The camp became known as Fort Mandan.

Mandan families gathered together inside their lodge.

October 1804	November 1804	December 1804
The Corps reaches a Mandan village	Lewis and Clark meet Sacagawea	The Corps completes Fort Mandan

Meeting Sacagawea

The winter was long and bitterly cold, with temperatures falling below −40°C (−40°F). To keep busy, the men went hunting with the Mandan and mended their tools. Time was also spent treating **frostbite** and other illnesses. One day, a French fur hunter, Toussaint Charbonneau, arrived at Fort Mandan. Lewis hired Charbonneau as an interpreter and guide. He agreed to let his Native American wife, Sacagawea, come along for the journey.

The harsh Missouri winter

Mandan villages

The Mandan were a Native American tribe who lived along the banks of the Missouri River. Traditionally, their villages were round, earth lodges arranged around a central square. Up to 30–40 people lived inside each lodge.

HIGHLIGHTS

Sacagawea belonged to the Shoshone tribe but had been **kidnapped** at the age of twelve by the Hidatse tribe. She lived in a Hidatse village, where she met and married Charbonneau. She quickly became an important member of the expedition. Afterwards, she and Charbonneau settled in St Louis. She died of a fever in 1812.

December 1804 – April 1805

The Corps spends winter
in Fort Mandan

1 January 1805

The Corps celebrates
New Year

The Great Falls

When spring came, Lewis and Clark sent some of the men back to St Louis with the keelboat. It was loaded with **specimens** of plants, animals, and rocks. Meanwhile, Lewis and Clark left Fort Mandan and headed west again.

Disaster strikes!

In May, the canoe carrying their precious books, medicines, and scientific instruments overturned. Luckily, Sacagawea acted quickly and rescued most of the items washed overboard.

The Rocky Mountains – covered with winter snow

April 1805	May 1805	June 1805
Lewis and Clark leave Fort Mandan	A canoe overturns in a storm	The Corps reaches the Great Falls

Lewis and Clark encountered deadly rattlesnakes along their route.

Around the Great Falls

In June, the expedition reached a fork in the river. Lewis and Clark decided to head south. A few days later, their way was blocked by a huge waterfall. It was impossible to cross by boat. Instead, they had to load the canoes on to carts and drag them around. Avoiding rattlesnakes, grizzly bears, and cacti, they reached safety but it had taken a whole month. They needed to cross the Rocky Mountains before winter, and they were running out of time.

June – July 1805

The Corps passes the
Great Falls

Late July 1805

The Corps reaches the
Three Forks of the Missouri

Crossing the Rockies

Beyond the Great Falls lay the towering Rockies. But Lewis and Clark needed horses to cross the mountains. Once again, Sacagawea came to their rescue.

Shoshone lands

The mountains were home to the Shoshone, Sacagawea's people. On meeting a group of Shoshone, Sacagawea recognized her brother, who was chief of the tribe. She had not seen him for many years. Her brother gave Lewis and Clark the horses and guides that they needed.

A chief of the Nez Perce Indians

August 1805	26 August 1805	13 September 1805
Lewis and Clark meet the Shoshone	Lewis crosses the Continental Divide	The Corps crosses the Lolo trail

A terrible trek

At the end of August, Lewis and Clark set out to cross the mountains. A terrible 11-day journey lay ahead. Thick forests blocked their path, and the weather was bitterly cold. With no animals to hunt, they quickly ran out of food and were forced to kill and eat their horses. Starving and exhausted, they eventually stumbled into a camp belonging to the Nez Perce Indians. The Indians brought them fish and roots to eat, and showed them which way to go.

WHAT THEY SAID:

"The mountains of the East [were] covered with snow. We met with a great misfortune, in having our last thermometer broken by accident. This day we passed over immense hills and some of the worst roads that ever horses passed. Our horses frequently fell."

Clark's diary, 3 September 1805

A Nez Perce camp and tribespeople. Lewis and Clark took shelter in a camp similar to this one.

September – October 1805

The Corps crosses the Rockies

October 1805

The Corps meet the Nez Perce

The Pacific

Once they were safely across the Rockies, Lewis and Clark set up camp on the banks of the Clearwater River. Here, the men rested before the last leg of their journey to the sea.

New canoes

With help from the Nez Perce, the men made new canoes from pine trees. Then they left their horses with the tribe, and set off along the Clearwater and Snake Rivers, until they reached the Columbia River. It was no easy ride. There were many **rapids** to get around, including the Grand Rapids – 8 kilometres (5 miles) of whirling water.

A Nez Perce tribesperson uses a pine tree canoe.

Early October 1805	16 October 1805	18 October 1805
The men make new canoes	The Corps reaches the Columbia River	Clark sees Mount Hood

River rapids are whirling masses of water that can easily overturn a boat.

WHAT THEY SAID:

Ocean view

On 7 November, Lewis and Clark reached a wide stretch of water which they believed to be the Pacific Ocean. They were actually in the **estuary** of the Columbia, still some 30 kilometres (18.5 miles) from the coast. Two weeks later, they finally reached the Pacific, and their goal.

"Great joy in camp. We are in view of the ocean, this great Pacific Ocean which we [have] been so long anxious to see. And the roaring or noise made by the waves breaking on the rocky shore may be heard distinctly."

Clark's diary, 7 November 1805

7 November 1805
The Corps reaches the Columbia estuary

24 November 1805
The Corps reaches the Pacific Ocean

Fort Clatsop

On reaching the Pacific, Lewis and Clark hoped to find a **trading ship** to take them home. But no ships sailed by and they were forced to spend another winter away from home.

Fort Clatsop

By now, the weather was terrible with fierce storms lashing the coast. Lewis went ahead by canoe to find a campsite. He chose a spot on the south side of the river, which was sheltered from the wind and rain. There the men set to work building their winter camp, which they called Fort Clatsop.

The Corps camp at Fort Clatsop

November 1805	December 1805	December 1805 – March 1806
The Corps vote where to build their camp	Fort Clatsop is completed	The Corps spends winter at Fort Clatsop

Winterwork

The Corps spent the winter getting ready for their journey home. Lewis and Clark caught up with writing their diaries, and making notes and maps. Meanwhile, the men went hunting for food, and made clothes and **moccasins** from elk skins. Despite the rain, they welcomed in the New Year with a meal of boiled elk, washed down with water.

Fort Clatsop had two rows of wooden huts, around a parade ground. There were rooms for Lewis and Clark, the men and for Sacagawea, Charbonneau, and their young son. The fort was named after the local Clatsop Native Americans.

Elks were hunted for their meat and skin.

December 1805 – March 1806	1 January 1806
The Corps make hundreds of pairs of mocassins	The Corps celebrates New Year

Homeward Bound

In March 1806, Lewis and Clark left Fort Clatsop and began their long journey home. All of their belongings were packed into six new canoes.

Nez Perce tribespeople lived in tents called tepees.

A difficult start

Strong **currents** and waterfalls made it difficult to sail back up the Columbia River. Lewis and Clark were forced to abandon their canoes. They collected their horses from the Nez Perce, but had to wait another month for the snow to melt before they could set off. In June, they were at last able to cross the Rockies and return to the Missouri River.

March 1806	May 1806	May – June 1806
The Corps leaves Fort Clatsop	The Corps reaches the Nez Perce camp	The Corps prepares to cross the Rockies

The only way to travel through the Rocky Mountains was on foot or on horseback.

Separate ways

After crossing the Rockies, Lewis and Clark decided to split the Corps into two teams. They wanted to gather more information about the region and make sure that they had not missed an easier river route to the Pacific.

HIGHLIGHTS

The Nez Perce are a Native American tribe that originally lived in the Pacific north-west region of the USA. They spent winter living in villages. In summer, they travelled around in search of buffalo and salmon to hunt. Without the help of the Nez Perce, Lewis and Clark's expedition might well have failed.

June 1806

The Corps crosses the Rockies again

3 July 1806

The Corps splits into two groups

A Final Skirmish

After splitting up, Lewis and his team headed north, while Clark went south. Each had many more adventures before they met up again.

Clark's journey

Travelling by horse and canoe, Clark headed down the Beaverhead and Yellowstone rivers to the Great Falls. He was amazed by the vast numbers of animals he saw. At one point, he had to wait for an hour for a huge herd of buffalo to cross the river. On the way, half of his horses were stolen by the Crow Indians and the rest went **lame**.

Lush forests surround the Beaverhead river.

July 1806	July 1806	15 July 1806
Clark explores the Yellowstone River	Lewis explores the Marias River	Lewis reaches Camp Disappointment

WHAT THEY SAID:

Lewis's journey

Meanwhile, Lewis set off to explore the Marias River but soon found himself in trouble. In a skirmish with some Blackfeet Indians over stolen guns and horses, two Blackfeet were killed. Lewis was forced to flee for his life. Later, a short-sighted hunter accidentally shot him in the leg and he spent several weeks on a stretcher.

"I was in the act of firing on the elk…when a [bullet] struck my left thigh…I instantly supposed that Cruzatte had shot me in mistake for an elk as I was dressed in brown leather and he cannot see very well."

Lewis's diary, 11 August 1806

Journey's End

The Corps met up again in August at the meeting point of the Yellowstone and Missouri rivers in North Dakota. They were now on the final leg of their journey home.

A sad farewell

Sailing down the Missouri, Lewis and Clark reached the Mandan villages again. There, they said goodbye to Sacagawea and Charbonneau. Later, Clark settled them in St Louis and helped to look after their children.

Many American coins and stamps show Lewis, Clark, and Sacagawea.

12 August 1806	14 August 1806	August 1806
Lewis and Clark meet up again	The Corps reaches the Mandan village	Sacagawea stays with the Mandan

President
Thomas
Jefferson

A hero's welcome

Lewis and Clark finally reached St Louis on 23 September 1806. They had covered 12,370 kilometres (nearly 7,700 miles) in just under two and a half years. Most people thought they were dead because they had not heard anything about them for many months. Soon afterwards, the Corps of Discovery was broken up. Lewis and Clark went on to Washington DC to report back to President Jefferson about the amazing sights they had seen.

WHAT THEY SAID:

"Sir,
It is with pleasure that I announce to you the safe arrival of myself and party at 12 o'clock today at this place with our papers and baggage. In accordance to your orders, we have penetrated the Continent of North America to the Pacific Ocean...."

Lewis's letter to President Jefferson, 23 September 1806

23 September 1806

The Corps reaches
St Louis

Autumn 1806

The Corps is
broken up

27

Lewis and Clark's Legacy

Although Lewis and Clark did not find an easy river route across the western USA, they brought back a huge amount of information about the region.

New discoveries

On their travels, Lewis and Clark discovered about 300 **species** of animals and plants that had not been known before. They also met many groups of Native Americans and described the Rocky Mountains. They wrote detailed notes of everything they saw in their diaries.

This page from Lewis and Clark's expedition diary shows a sketch of a newly-discovered bird.

1807	11 October 1809	1813
Lewis is appointed Governor of Louisiana	Lewis dies	Clark is appointed Governor of Missouri

This is one of the expedition maps made by Lewis and Clark

Later life

President Jefferson rewarded Lewis and Clark with government jobs and land. Clark became Governor of Missouri, then **Superintendent** of Indian Affairs. He married twice and had eight children. He died in 1838.

Lewis was appointed Governor of Louisiana but was accused of doing his job badly. In 1809, he died of gunshot wounds on his way to Washington DC to clear his name. Most people believe that he killed himself. Others thought that he had been murdered.

HIGHLIGHTS

Lewis and Clark made many maps of the north-west USA. The maps showed, for the first time, the correct locations of the Columbia and the Missouri rivers, and the Rocky Mountains.

1822	1 September 1838
Clark is put in charge of Indian Affairs	Clark dies

Glossary

biology study of living things

blacksmiths people who make objects from iron, such as horseshoes

currents flow of a river

dysentery serious illness of the intestines

elk large deer, also called a moose

estuary marshy area where a river flows into the sea

expedition journey or voyage of exploration

frostbite when flesh gets so cold that it freezes and turns black

interpreter person who translates from one language into another

keelboat flat-bottomed boat

kidnap to carry someone off against their will

lame having damaged or weak feet

moccasins shoes made from soft leather

Native American people who lived in North America before settlers arrived from other countries

navigation the skill of plotting a route

private secretary person who looks after the affairs of an important official, such as a president

rapids part of a river where the water is very fast and rough

rodents animals, such as squirrels, rats, and mice

sandbars ridges of sand in a river

skirmish short fight between two sides

species types of animals or plants

specimens plants and animals studied for scientific research

superintendant person in charge

trading ship ship that carries goods from one place to another

Further Information

Websites

Follow Lewis and Clark's journey at:
www.nationalgeographic.com/lewisandclark

Find out about the discoveries made by Lewis and Clark at:
www.lewis-clark.org

Read more about the expedition at:
www.lewisandclark.org

Books

Across America: The Lewis and Clark Expedition by Maurice Isserman. Chelsea House Publishers (2009).

How We Crossed the West by Meriwether Lewis and William Clark. National Geographic Books (1997).

Places to visit

Fort Mandan (reconstruction), Washburn, North Dakota, USA.

Fort Clatsop National Memorial, Astoria, Oregon, USA.

Lewis and Clark Boat House and Nature Center, St Charles, Missouri, USA.

Index